How do werewolves like their eggs cooked?

Terror-fried.

What happened when the werewolf swallowed a clock?

He got ticks.

What does a vampire use to clean his house?

A victim cleaner.

Why does Dracula have no friends?

He's a pain in the neck.

What's a vampire's favourite sweet?

One he can suck.

What does a vampire fear the most?

Tooth decay.

14

What is a zombie's favourite food?

Baked brains.

Who won the zombie football match?

No one, it was dead even.

What is a mummy's favourite type of music?

Wrap.

What kind of girl does a mummy take on a date?

Any girl he can dig up.

Skeletons in the closet

What happens to clumsy ghosts?

They get cuts and boosies.

Where do young ghosts go during the day?

Dayscare centres.

When does a ghost
have breakfast?

In the moaning.

What's a ghost's
favourite fruit?

**Boo-berry pie
with I-scream.**

Who won the skeleton beauty contest?

No body.

Why didn't the skeleton cross the road?

Because he didn't have the guts.

Further reading

Monster Jokes (Practical Joke Books),
Clare Trotman (Top That! Publishing, 2007)

The Monster Joke Book, Shoo Rayner
(Collins Educational, 2007)

Create your own joke

Follow these steps to write your own joke:

1. Pick two topics. One-word nouns are good.
   For example, "bee" and "transport".

2. Make a list of words connected to your topics
   - "hive", "nest", "buzz", and "bus", "train", "boat".

3. Make a list of joke types. For example:
   "What do you call a ..."
   "How does a ..."

4. Try out different jokes, fitting your words from step
   2 into the joke types from step 3. For example,
   "How does a bee get to work?" "By buzz!"